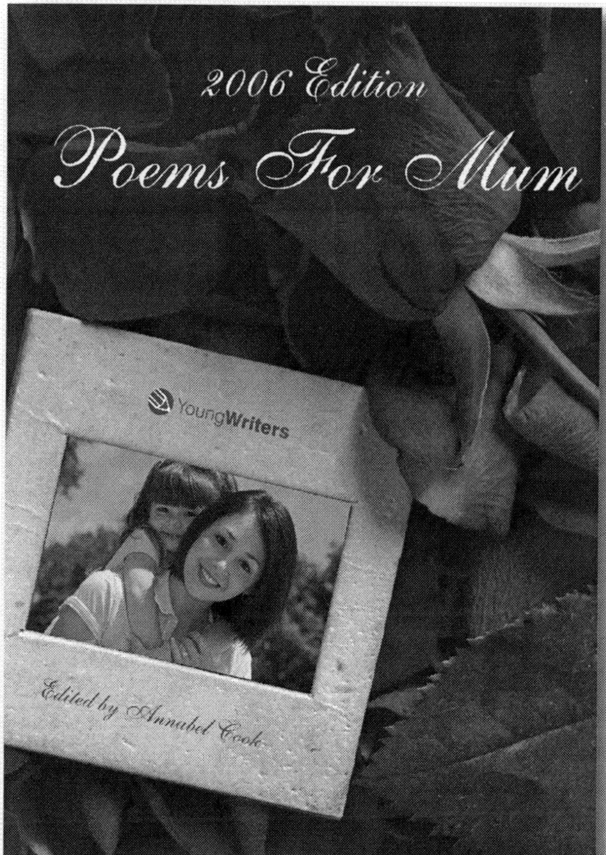
2006 Edition
Poems For Mum
YoungWriters
Edited by Annabel Cook

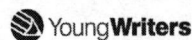

First published in Great Britain in 2006 by:
Young Writers
Remus House
Coltsfoot Drive
Peterborough
PE2 9JX
Telephone: 01733 890066
Website: www.youngwriters.co.uk
All Rights Reserved
© Copyright Contributors 2006
SB ISBN 1-84602-370-X

Disclaimer
Young Writers has maintained every effort
to publish stories that will not cause offence.
Any stories, events or activities relating to individuals
should be read as fictional pieces and not construed
as real-life character portrayal.

Foreword

This anthology contains a collection of verse dedicated to one of the most remarkable and influential people in our lives – our mum. All of the poems within this book have been written by young people and convey their appreciation for all the fantastic things their mums have done for them. Originally sent in as entries for a Mother's Day poetry competition the following pages contain those entries that have been handpicked as the best of the bunch. This special selection begins with the winning entry, *Mothers Are Like Flowers*, by Briony Steele.

Contents

Briony Steele (12)	9
Taylor Pollock (12)	10
Shannon Russell (12)	11
Gavin Ludlow (11)	12
David McGibbon (11)	13
Michael Morrow (12)	14
Heather Agnew (11)	15
Sarah Bingham (11)	16
Andrew Clarke (12)	17
Julia Hinds (11)	18
Hannah Brennan (12)	19
Niamh Blackburn (11)	20
Shanaide Robinson (12)	21
Anam Ashraf (13)	22
Laurent Vaughan (10)	23
Aimee Lee (11)	24
Natasha Oliver-Smith (12)	25
Alicia Munro (10)	26
Imogen Langton (10)	27
Rachel Stone (9)	28
Rochelle Logan-Rodgers (17)	29
Andrew Bradley (11)	30
Andrew Flack (11)	31
Jemima Brown (12)	32
Rachel Braniff (12)	33
Ryan McNaney (11)	34
Kirsty McGregor-Ritchie (13)	35
Saoirse O'Loughlin (9)	36
Tonicha Stroud (8)	37
Andrew Anderson (9)	38
Katie McCallum (12)	39
Natasha Cheung (12)	40
Rachel Grashion (9)	41
Gurpreet Bharya (15)	42
Lauren Simmons (10)	43
Claire Thompson (12)	44
Leanne Spry (11)	45
Chorin Kawa (15)	46
Macauley Thornton (8)	47
Erin Weston (13)	48
Chamelle Davies (13)	49
Madeeha Chowdhury (12)	50
Jade Edwards (13)	51
Tamsin Taylor (14)	52
Rachel Pentland (13)	53
Chloe O'Carroll (12)	54
Emma Frost (11)	55
Aimee Hadman (12)	56
Matthew Pickering (13)	57
Aysha Iqbal (11)	58
Freya Chappell (10)	59
Gurvinder Bhangal (8)	60
Charlie Emsley (13)	61
Ella McEwen (12)	62
Alice Zapparova (12)	63
Lucy Rolli (11)	64
Truth St Louis (10)	65
Laura Edwards (12)	66
Natalie Howard (14)	67
Lydia Shore (12)	68
Kate Parsons (11)	69
Kajal Patel (11)	70
Anna Lightfoot (12)	71
Paul Aitchison (13)	72
Rachel Star (9)	73
Natalie Elizabeth Steinmetz (12)	74
Comfort Nwabia (12)	75
Sophie Walters (12)	76
Nicole Holmes (12)	77
Cassandra Nelson (13)	78
Katy Furness (13)	79
Katie Lord (12)	80
Tansy B Grady (15)	81
Laura Caldwell (11)	82
Amy Down (12)	83
Michelle Bailey (14)	84
Radhaika Kumari Kapur (12)	85
Iqra Aslam (11)	86
Faye Clayton (11)	87
Alex Drake (11)	88
Lucy Pullinger (10)	89
Lauren Garbett (10)	90
Michael Johnston (15)	91
Jodie O'Donnell (14)	92
Natalie Robson (11)	93
Kirsty Rollason (14)	94
Joshua Everett (10)	95
Josephine Goh (9)	96
Leonie Reed (15)	97
Chelsea Butler (8)	98
Hannah Bolt (9)	99
Sammi-Jo Ward (12)	100
Amun Bal (11)	101
Rosie Grieve (9)	102
Rachel Stanley (11)	103
Sarah Jane Simpson (16)	104
Clare Stevens (10)	105
Jess Teggart (13)	106

Name	Page
Cindel Simmill (14)	107
Chloe Schofield (9)	108
Katie Schofield (9)	109
Jonathan Venus (9)	110
Rosanna Bucknill (10)	111
Abbie Mitchell (11)	112
Charlotte Morris (13)	113
Daisy Maria Harvey (11)	114
Rebecca Parker (9)	115
Punika Kotecha (10)	116
Samantha Croal (12)	117
Deva Edwards (12)	118
Rebecca Oborne (13)	119
Phoebe Wall (11)	120
Rebekah Fenwick (10)	121
Katy Morgan (11)	122
Ellie McIntyre (10)	123
Victoria Rostock (13)	124
Sam Martin Watts (9)	125
Melanie Rayner (12)	126
Vicky Adelmant (11)	127
Helena Eccles (11)	128
Eleanor Easton (11)	129
Gemma Altham (13)	130
Nicole Petrillo (12)	131
Jigar Patel (13)	132
Jessica Copland (14)	133
Mica Sinforiani (11)	134
Katherine Hill (12)	135
Emma Atkinson (12)	136
Catrin Davies (11)	137
Louise Balloch (11)	138
Erin Considine (11)	139
Alicja Borsberry-Woods (11)	141
Jessica Bennett (11)	142
Ashley Dodds (11)	143
Margaret Coleman (11)	144
Clare Carr (11)	145
Suzy Davenport (12)	146
Bethan Dalby (11)	147
Regan Everson (10)	148
Niall Cullen (10) & Declan Hirrell (7)	149
Anthony Thomas	150
Chelsea Hill (11)	151
Tayla Houston (10)	152
Courtney Wallace (10)	153
Jade Evans (10)	154
Katie Heapy (10)	155
Craig Kinsella (10)	156
Liam Carpenter (9)	157
Jazzmin Robinson (10)	158
Liberty Edler Davies (10)	159
Billy Elsey (9)	160
Danny Dabin (9)	161
Joshua White (9)	162
Carly Stone (9)	163
Amelia Clark (9)	164
Hannah Lee (9)	165
Charlotte Wakefield (9)	166
April Walker	167
Abigail Goodwin (9)	168
Libby Smith	169
Tyler Barrow (9)	170
James Kose (9)	171
Danny O'Halloran (9)	172
Harry Webster (9)	173
Lara Leyser (9)	174
Ryan Simmons (10)	175
Charlie-Boy Howard	176
Dawn Ellis (14)	177
Thomas Bartos (9)	178
Elizabeth Ashamu (8)	179
Daniella Graham (8)	180
Nana-Akyere Quagraine (8)	181
Hamza Osman (8)	182
Chloe O'Dwyer (9)	183
Daniela Saramago (8)	184
Chanice Nembhard (8)	185
Timi Akinyemi (8)	186
Berya Mehmet (9)	187
Laura Aimable (8)	188
Denzil Sampson (8)	189
Bobi Jean Benjamin (8)	190
Raphael Anene (8)	191
Patrice McLynn (8)	192
Sylvia Anyan-Brown (9)	193
Brittany Dawson	194
Saffron McGibbon (9)	195
Adnan Sakinsel (8)	196
Canan Kolcak (8)	197
Jordan Messoud	198
Shadia Hussain (10)	199
Rachel Cable (11)	200
Abigail Cotton (11)	201
Emma Cook (11)	202
Amy Brown (12)	203
Sinead Cleaver (11)	204
Sana Chaudhry (12)	205
Hannah Bradford (11)	206
Catherine Bowering (11)	207
Amy Breakwell (12)	208
Rosie Dowd-Smyth (11)	209
Madeeha Ahmed (16)	210
Young Writers Information	212

The Poems

Mothers Are Like Flowers

Mothers are like flowers
They are all original,
All beautiful in their own way
They are bright and lovely
To cheer you up in times of sadness
They are never dull or grey
Forever in their prime

Mothers are like trees
Whether you do right or wrong,
They are always there to love you
They stay rooted in the ground,
Helping you through the stormiest of times
They conceal you from danger,
Protecting you from the world

Mothers are like flowers
They are all original,
All beautiful in their own way
And however many are grown
In a world of fields
There is also one who knows you
And will love you for evermore.

Briony Steele (12)

Congratulations Briony. Your lovely poem was our favourite in this collection and wins you a beautiful bouquet of flowers which will be delivered to your mum in time for Mother's Day. Well done.

Mother's Day Poem

Mummy, oh Mummy I love you more each day,
This is something I cannot say,
I have tried to remember to tell you this 'cause it's true,
Mummy, oh Mummy I do love you!

Lying in bed gazing at the stars,
Trying to remember all our happy hours,
Sometimes I dream about them too,
Mummy, oh Mummy I do love you!

When I was a baby you listened to my cries,
But you were always there to dry my eyes,
You have always been there for me when I've needed you,
Mummy, oh Mummy I do love you.

You helped me take my first steps and heard my first words,
You took me on my first day of school,
And helped me learn how to spell, write and read too,
Mummy, oh Mummy I do love you.

When it is just you and me watching TV
You'd look at the picture of me when I was wee,
Then you would look over at me and say,
I wish I could have you back like that for one more day!

Mummy, oh Mummy I do love you
I have written this poem just to show you,
I think this is special for me to say,
I am increasing my love for you each day!

I will always love you for evermore,
I will remember to tell you this each day,
From the bottom of my heart I mean every word I say,
Mummy, oh Mummy I love you so much it's untrue,
Mummy, oh Mummy I do love you!

Taylor Pollock (12)

Mother's Day

M is for *my* mum, the best mum in the world.
O is for mums living all *over* the world.
T is for *they* will always love you.
H is they could never and will never *hate* you.
E is for your mum who does *everything* to make sure you're happy and safe.
R is for your mum who makes sure everything is *ready* for you.
S is for my mum, she is a *saint*.

D is for *don't* ever do anything bad to your mum.
A is for *always* love your mum.
Y is for *your* mum who is the most special person to you ever.

Shannon Russell (12)

Thanks Mum

This poem is dedicated to you,
Because you taught me to say please and thank you,
So now I'm saying thanks for all that you do.

When I wake up you are there,
Telling me to get dressed and tidy my hair,
From first thing in the morning I know that you care.

When I go to bed at night
I know you've helped make my day alright.

You look after my health,
Saying it's more important than wealth.

You make sure I'm safe and well
And if I go out you make me tell.

You watch and make sure I don't fall,
I think you're the best mum overall.

You're always there to help me out,
It's not that often I would hear you shout.

You want me to grow up to be a good man,
I want you to know I'm your number one fan!

You teach me to do my best at school,
Mum I think you really rule.

You want me to be happy not sad,
You want me to be good not bad.

You're always a good laugh and have fun,
I love you because you're a great mum.

The fact that you'll even pick up my dirty socks
Proves to me that my mum rocks!

Gavin Ludlow (11)

Mum

My mother is a housewife,
Her favourite colour's green.
Hoovering, cleaning, tidying,
Mum tries to keep me clean.

My mother has got brown hair,
Mum's got blue eyes as well.
Short yet strong and bubbly,
Mum often works pell-mell.

A driver, gardener, shopper,
A doctor, listener, friend.
A teacher, helper, carer,
Mum also likes to mend.

Mum likes to talk with people
And do a little sport.
Mum doesn't like bad language,
Or when we misbehave.

David McGibbon (11)

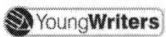

A Poem About My Mum

Mum, without you I would not be on planet Earth,
So it seems unfair you had my very painful birth,
You watched me grow up
And supported what I did,
And let me have independence,
Even though I was just a kid,
You made my dinner almost every night,
And told me if I ate my greens I'd get bigger in height,
On my first day of primary school you told me you had to leave,
I wouldn't let you go and held on to your sleeve,
You had three children to deal with,
You did it well,
Even though you always threatened to throw us off a cliff,
When it came to the 11+ you said it wouldn't matter if I got a V,
Because I'm your son and you still love me,
Saying thank you is the least I can say,
I love you Mum, so have a brilliant Mother's Day.

Michael Morrow (12)

A Poem For Mum

My mum is the greatest mum of them all
She looked after me since before I could crawl
She taught me how to use the potty
And then eventually the lavatory
If I had a nightmare she'd hold me tight
And tuck me up and say goodnight
I'm glad she's part of my family tree
I love her and she loves me!

Heather Agnew (11)

My Mum

My mum is really brill
She has a lot to do
She looks after Dad and me
And copes with her job too

She goes shopping at Tesco
Every single Sunday
She fills her trolley up to the brim
And spends a lot of money

She takes me out for treats
On weekends and at holidays
She's always there to have a chat
And gives me pocket money

Mum is a great driver
But she is a crazy parker
When she's finally chosen a space
God help the cars beside her

Thank you my dear mother
For everything you've done
To me you truly are
The whole world's greatest mum.

Sarah Bingham (11)

Mum Poem

Mum I don't know how to start
To tell you what is in my heart.

I find it hard to say
How much I love you day by day.

You always help me to do my best
And praise me when I pass each test.

You make our home a place of light
With your presence warm and bright.

I know I was your baby boy
And that I brought you lots of joy.

You have been my guide,
I hope to make your heart fill with pride.

Andrew Clarke (12)

My Mum

My mum, a busy bee
My mum, a mummy to me!
Rushing in, rushing out,
Rushing around and all about.
My mummy always has time for me.

Working here, working there
Always working but always there!

A mummy of four means lots of chores
And many mummies would shout, 'No more!'
Not my mummy, she shouts all the more.

My mummy is fab, my mummy is chill,
My mummy is cool, my mummy is brill.

My mummy's the greatest, my mummy's the best,
My mummy's my mummy and always the best!

Julia Hinds (11)

Thank You Mum

Thank you Mum, you are so sweet
Thank you Mum, you keep me neat
Thank you Mum, without a doubt
You are the best mum about.

Thank you Mum, when I am sad
Thank you Mum, you make me glad
Thank you Mum, without a doubt
You are the best mum about.

Thank you Mum, you're always there
Thank you Mum, you always care
Thank you Mum, without a doubt
You are the best mum about.

Thank you Mum, you are a dime
Thank you Mum, one last time
Thank you Mum, without a doubt
You are the best mum about.

Hannah Brennan (12)

The Best Mum Ever

The best mum ever would ...
Make your breakfast, lunch and dinner
Give you all the love, care and everything she can afford.

> The best mum ever would ...
> Stick up for you
> And be there for you when you are lonely.

The best mum ever would ...
Buy you everything you need and give
And buy you treats
Give you pocket money when she can.

> The best mum ever would ...
> Never make fun of you or laugh at you,
> Or if you had a bad hair day she would fix it.

The best mum ever would ...
Sacrifice anything for you
And ... *the best mum ever ... is my mum.*

Niamh Blackburn (11)

Poem For Mum

My mum's love is like a red boat floating in a tunnel full of love,
God must have sent her from above.
She turns me up when I am down,
Her love just keeps on turning me round.
Her singing sounds like the birds singing in the tree
And she smells so nice that she smells like honey bees.
I will love my mum whatever happens,
Because I know she always loves me.

Shanaide Robinson (12)

I Love You Mum And Thank You!

'Mum don't go!'
As she left me ...
Whispers of the night awoke me
Then I realised ...
How much she meant to me.

She is always happy
Which makes me smile
I could do anything for her
Even run that last mile!

My mum is something wonderful
She makes me feel all warm inside
My mum is friendly, special and kind
She is in my heart
And she is always on my mind.

I really love my mum
The thoughts of her -
Fill me with pride!

But sometimes I stop and think ...
Do I deserve my mum?
Do I appreciate her?
Someone to talk to
Someone to listen to

Have I ever stopped to thank my mum?
It hurts when I think that I haven't now ...
I just wish ...
My mum would never leave me again.

'I love you Mum and thank you!'

Adam Ashraf (13)

Poem For Mum

My mum is the sweetest thing
She sparkles in the night
Like a diamond ring
Always doing something
Cooking, washing
Taking us to school
I don't know about you lot
But I think my mum is really cool
She is the heart of the family
The flames of the sun
The core of the forest
She is the best and only one
    My mum.

Laurent Vaughan (10)

My Mum

The special person is my mum
She makes me laugh; we have so much fun,
She helps me get my homework done.
My mum keeps me warm in the bitter
And helps me sprinkle a lot of glitter,
She hates loads of litter.
My mum has got black hair,
Brown eyes and white teeth
And she loves lots of beef,
Now you know about my mum,
She helps me fill my little tum.

Aimee Lee (11)

The One Who Cares

Out of all the people in the world,
I have the best mum,
Mums aren't just here to cook and clean,
They're here for lots of fun.

My mum helps me if I need help,
Or gives me great advice.
She takes me out on shopping sprees
And in return I'm very nice.

If I'm in trouble at school
Or am not feeling too well,
Mum tells me not to worry
Because I'm her eldest girl.

Sometimes I argue with my mum,
But it's best not to hold a grudge.
We say our sorrys for what we did,
Then I tuck into some fudge.

My mum can be strict sometimes,
But I understand why.
But other children don't
So they have a good old cry.

But is this really necessary?
Because mums try to keep you safe.
So try to compromise the problem
And try to keep her faith.

So if you think your mum is strict,
It's just because she cares.
Poor orphans don't even have a mum
To be ungrateful is not fair.

So I just want to say
That Mum, I love you
And even if I don't show it sometimes
I always will and always do.

Natasha Oliver-Smith (12)

Poem For Mum

Picks me up and takes me there,
Full of love and bursting with care.
Hot dinner waiting after school,
Chases fashion and looks so cool.
Helps with homework if I'm stuck,
Before a match she gives me luck.
Standing, cheering, by my side,
She always fills my heart with pride.
So thank you Mum, I'm glad you're mine
Snazzy, loving, all the time.

Alicia Munro (10)

Big Thank You Mum

Thank you for giving me advice for school
Thank you for helping me to swim like a dolphin
Thank you for doing me sausages and chicken nuggets for packed lunch
Thank you for being there through the bad times
Thank you for making every birthday a birthday I can't forget
My friends think you are cool
'Cause you're my mum.

Imogen Langton (10)

Mum

There's someone special,
Who's my best friend
And I know we'll be friends,
To the very end.

She gave me my first hug
And heard my very first word,
She helped me walk on the living room rug
And helped me with memorable events that occurred.

So who is this person
You may be asking?
Who is this person
Who seems multitasking?

With this person
I have a friendship which is true.
So to my mum I say,
Thank you!

Rachel Stone (9)

Happy Mother's Day

Dedicated to Patricia S Rodgers

My sweet, beautiful mother
I love you so much
To me there is no other
Who possesses that gentle touch.

You brought me into this world
Of pain and suffering
I'm glad I'm your favourite girl
Because you're caring and loving.

I am your daughter
As thankful to God as can be
You are my mother
A cinnamon, buzzing queen bee.

Our bond is so strong
Forever it will stay
It continues to grow long
Strengthening day by day.

You're so intelligent and smart
I miss your company while you're away
So imaginative and full of art
Happy Mother's Day.

Rochelle Logan-Rodgers (17)

Mom Poem

You have filled my life with joy
Ever since I was a boy
You have helped me learn things
Even when the phone rings

You have bought me toys and games
And helped me on my way to fame
You go to keep fit
Though you look like a twit

You are a teacher
And shout like a loud creature
You will always be there
No matter where.

Andrew Bradley (11)

My Mum

Dedicated to Valerie Flack

She works and works
from dusk till dawn
she tidies up the house
and mows the lawn.
From when we get up in the morning
and go to bed at night
she always has the house
sparkling bright.
If I work in the morning
I like to get paid
and if I don't
I just go back to bed.

Andrew Flack (11)

Why Mums Are So Important

Our mums are not only brilliant
They're really helpful too,
They make you dinner every night
And buy you pressies so they do,
Even if you fight,
Yell, roar and scream,
She'll always love you no matter what,
Maybe even more than ice cream,
If you're stuck on something,
Homework or your friends,
She'll be sure to help you,
And you'll conquer it in the end,
Your mum is so important,
Talk to her every day,
About problems, needs and doubts
Don't you worry,
She'll help you in every way.

Jemima Brown (12)

A Poem Dedicated To My Mum

My mum is special
My mum is unique
Never mind birthdays or Christmas
We dance all week.

> She loves to go shopping
> To see what is there!
> Clothes, bags, shoes
> She doesn't really care!

But that is not all
My mum can do
She works and works
The whole day through.

> But most important of all
> And I know it's true
> She cares and loves
> And sees me through.

Rachel Braniff (12)

My Mum

Mum runs around looking after us
Always keeping time, never makes a fuss.

She always has me entertained
No chance of ever getting caned.

She's very loving and gives us care
Goes to the shops and buys us clothes to wear.

She nurses me when I'm feeling ill
She's always at hand with a pill.

Mum comforts me and wipes my tears
When she's there, I have no fears.

She always keeps me on the go
And really hates me being slow.

She's generous and kind and there's always laughter
She or my dad, I don't know who's dafter!

Mum's always rushing, she makes me dizzy
That's because she's always busy.

I walk into the bathroom, oh she's nude
I think that is very rude!

She's my mum, I think she's great
She is really my best mate.

Ryan McNaney (11)

My Mum

Precious ... lovely ... kind ... funny ... caring

The only person in the world
That listens and understands me properly.

When tears are rolling down my face,
I clear my eyes and see a smiling, caring face -
And see my mum!

My mum is not just there for me when times are tough
And going through rough times a teenage girl goes through
But the fun times, a mother and daughter have!

Getting ready for parties,
Buying the most gorgeous clothes,
Watching the coolest films; stuffing our faces with chocolate!
Shopping, painting our nails ...
My mum also does not so glamorous things for me -
Like watching me race; even if it's in the wind, snow, rain or sun!
She is the one person I can count on to be there!

I love my mum millions - and hope everyone has a mum like mine.
Caring, lovely, funny
And the most precious person in my life!

Kirsty McGregor-Ritchie (13)

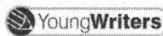

My Mum

I love my mum, she is cool
She really is a funny fool.
Her eyes are green and her hair is red
She's very very fond of bed.
She likes to read a good love book
And she is a brilliant cook.
She cooks us really lovely dinners
And tells us all that we are winners.
I love it when she gives me praise
And gives my pocket money a raise.
When we go shopping she buys me sweets
And sometimes we get extra treats.
In the house she does lots of jobs
Picking up our bits and bobs.
She always does her very best
And then she needs a good long rest.
I really love my lovely mum
She is my extra special chum.

Saoirse O'Loughlin (9)

My Mum's Story

Thank you Mum for being the best,
But now I think you're in need of a rest,
You wash and iron all day long,
But I tell you that is so wrong.
Thank you for looking after me and Madison,
And here is a reward for what you've done.
Thank you for always being there for me,
And I will never swap you for anyone else,
Because you are simply the *best*.

Tonicha Stroud (8)

My Mum

My mum is good
My mum is special
My mum is funny
My mum helps me with my homework
My mum takes me out places
My mum plays games with me
My mum is always there when I hurt myself
My mum loves me and *I love my mum.*

Andrew Anderson (9)

My Mum

My mum is very good to me,
She buys me things I like!
But when I'm very naughty,
She calls me a little tike!

My mum takes me to nice places,
Of which I'm very pleased!
I have to take my sisters,
Who I like to aggravate and tease!

My mum likes me to do some chores,
And I really don't like cleaning floors!
But if I am given half a chance,
I would rather sing and dance!

This is when she shouts a lot,
But I am still grateful for the mum I've got!
She is the best mum to me,
I can remember when she bounced me on her knee!

This is what I'd like to say,
And this is for your special day!

Katie McCallum (12)

My Mum Is The One ...

My mum is the one who made me exist,
My mum is the one who watched me grow.
My mum is the one who cared for me.
My mum is the one who was there when I was ill.
My mum is the one to give me my pill.
She's the one always on my mind.

My mum is the one who cooked like a star,
My mum is the one who gave me a head start.
My mum was the one who taught me manners.
My mum is the one who taught me to read,
My mum is the one who showed me great patience.
She's the one always on my mind.

My mum is the one who showed me success,
My mum is the one who helped me get good grades.
My mum is the one who told me to do my homework,
My mum is the one who showed me the way.
My mum is the one who you could talk to, any day.
She's the one always on my mind.

My mum is the one who's better than the rest!
She was the one who helped me here,
To show me how to love each day,
Now I cherish you forever in my heart!

Natasha Cheung (12)

My Mum

T hank you Mum for always being there for me,
H elping me and caring for me,
A lthough we may fight, I will always care for you
N ever knowing how much you care for me,
K ind and caring, truthful and daring,

Y ou'll see in the way she sticks up for me,
O h this is a message I'm sending to you,
U nder my heart I feel for you.

Rachel Grashion (9)

Mum

Mum,
You are the world,
That I see,
Through the eyes
You gave me.

The light in every dark,
In every day,
In every night,

When you're there to say goodnight,
And wake up,
To take me here and there,
When I am unwell.

You are the reason that
I am strong,
All those times that I have done wrong,
I am sorry.

Although I have never told you,
Remember that I love you,
And that without you
I would not be here today.

You will always be in the best place in my heart,
The pillar to my life,
You know that I could not do
Without you.

Gurpreet Bharya (15)

Our Marvellous Mums

Dedicated to Christine Simmons

Mums are special, mums are unique,
Mums are the best brilliant treat!
Short or tall, black or white, fat or thin,
One of them is special to you!
Mums are special, mums are unique,
Mums are the best brilliant treat!
My mum does it all,
Cooks, cleans, irons, washes our clothes
And much more!
I love you!

Lauren Simmons (10)

My Mum

My mum is always there for me,
She cooks and cleans for me,
She helps me when I've hurt my knee,
My mum is always there for me.

My mum always cares about me,
She puts on a brave face for me,
She always tries to be funny,
My mum always cares about me.

My mum always loves me,
She always tries to help me,
She is always filled with empathy,
My mum always loves me.

So all in all, my mum is always there for me,
She always cares about me, she always loves me,
My mum is the greatest mum in history,
So you see, my mum is always there for me.

Claire Thompson (12)

Mum

Mum
You're always there for me through thick and thin
Cleaning up, cooking dinner and washing clothes
It's a tough life being a mum but you manage it and I appreciate it
When me and Ryan are throttling each other
You just want to vanish and burst into tears
But you stand your ground and lose your voice
Instead of shouting at us.
As a toddler you cleaned up my grazed knees
And as years went on you watched me start my first day at school,
And now my first day at secondary school.
You've watched me grow up to become a young adult
We can now go shopping together and have a girly night out,
Also share each other's shoes and clothes.
Thank you for being such a cool mum!
I feel I am one of the luckiest girls on Earth
To have a mum like you
You deserve a rest so relax and put your feet up
Let Dad do the dirty work for a while!

Leanne Spry (11)

Just A Thought

There is a thought that is disturbing me,
I keep wondering what my life would be like without my mummy.
I guess there would be a lot of pain and suffering,
It must make you wanna stop caring and living.

My cousin has been through it all,
For him it was a long, aggravating and desolate fall.
It left him weak, desperate and petrified,
He hallucinated for years and his eyes have never dried.

The nightmare continued inside my head,
As I battled such an infuriating concept.
Until I finally had to consult my cousin,
And ask what it felt like to be an orphan.

He turned to me and said;
What is a garden like without any roses?
What is the day like without the sun?
What is the night like without any stars?
What are you like without your heart?

I didn't have any answer to any of these,
But I still got the message,
How lucky am I to be blessed with an angel,
And if she were ever to fly away,
I would feel my heart rip and decay on that very day.

Chorin Kawa (15)

Mum

My mum is nice and calm like a dolphin,
She shouts like a lion,
She buys me surprises at Christmas,
And I love her.

My mum helps me with my homework,
She takes me to fun places,
She makes me laugh when I'm sad,
And I love her.

My mum helps me with my baking,
She takes me on holiday,
She looks after me when I'm ill,
And I love her.

Macauley Thornton (8)

My Mum

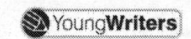

My mum is like a red, red rose,
Smelling sweet and pure.
My mum is like a love doctor,
That always finds a cure.
My mum is like a shining star,
Lighting up the clear night sky.
My mum is like a fluffy cloud,
Swaying way up high.
My mum is like my best friend,
My love for her will never end.
There'll never be another,
My one and only mother.

Erin Weston (13)

My Mam

My mam's my mam, friend, my heart and soul.
She gives me unconditional love as any other mum knows,
Her advice she gives without condemnation,
She opens her heart for me with lots of affection.

She grabs my hand for all to see,
That I'm her child no matter what I'll always be,
I'm never lonely as I've got my mam,
I really feel for those who have none.

She's taught me to love and understand,
Right from wrong, as we are always in command,
She gives me hope and her sincerity too,
Through all my challenges she'll see me through.

I've thought what life would be without my mam,
I pray and hope that day will never come,
But, if and when it's time to say goodbye,
I just want to curl up and die.

My mam says life will go on, in all of us, so please be strong,
Don't think like that, as you know it's wrong,
I'll always be with you come rain or shine,
I'll love you in death as in life, as you'll always be mine.

Chamelle Davies (13)

What Are Mums For?

What are mums for?
Mum is someone you love for being there when you need her.
She is full of warmth and fairness.
A mum is someone that you can trust
And she understands you in ups and downs.

A mum has confidence for your dreams to come true
And plans for the future.
She is always there, for thoughtful things to show she cares,
For making every day a special one!

A mum is for filling your life with love and happiness.

They are always special to your heart!
She should get love from everyone no matter what!
She is always there when you're sad or happy.

A mum is shared with everyone!
They make every day a special one!

A mum ... everyone has one!

Madeeha Chowdhury (12)

My Mum

All you have to do is see
Then you will agree
My mum is the best mum
We all want her to be
When she sees we are being bullied
She always helps me.
So I would like to say
Mum, thanks for being wonderful
In all the things you do.
You make the world a better place
Just by being you.
Thank you
You're special in each and every way
Thanks for all your love and support.

Jade Edwards (13)

My Mam

My mam is like a ray of sunshine to me.
She looks like an angel.
She is always there
Through the bad times of life.
She is like the stars shining in the night sky.
That is what I think of my mam.

That is my mam,
She is the best mam that anyone could wish for.
She is also my best friend
I love her so much.

Tamsin Taylor (14)

My Mum

My mum is someone special
She always makes my tea
When I get cold or flu
My mum looks after me.

My mum and I go to town
We both do like to shop
We browse among the bargain rails
And shop until we drop!

My mum is always happy
I love my mum no end
Not only is my mum, my mum
She's also my best friend.

Rachel Pentland (13)

My Mum

My mummy's wonderful,
I must say,
She's practically perfect,
In every way.

She never gets angry,
She never gets mad,
She loves me lots,
As well as my dad.

She couldn't do any more,
Even if she tried,
She's always there for me,
Always on my side.

That's my mum,
In a nutshell,
And all I want to do is yell ...
I love my mom!

Chloe O'Carroll (12)

Mum

Mum I just wanted to say thank you for:
The way you've looked after me for years
The way you've supported me
The way you've helped me do things I can't do alone.

I want to say thank you for:
The things you've bought me
And for the things you've done for me.

I want to say thank you for
The Hallowe'en and birthday parties you've done for me.

Mum you've done everything for me and I'm pleased
Of you, you're the best mum in the world.

Thank you for everything!

Emma Frost (11)

My Mum

My mum is the best,
She is better than the rest.

My mum likes to cook
And she likes to read a book.

My mum likes to read magazines
And she likes to wear jeans.

My mum helps walk the dogs
Even when the sky is full of fog.

Me and my mum like to make a cake
That's because we like to bake.

My mum is the best,
She is better than the rest.

Aimee Hadman (12)

Mum

Five, six, seventeen,
Nine, eleven, twenty-three,
Whatever age I might have been,
You've been through it all with me.

From when I was alive in you,
You've nurtured me and carried me through,
You helped me in the early years,
You shared my joy and wiped my tears.

And even as I'm getting older,
You're always there to pick me up,
Always been there for me,
Always been my loving mum,
My helping hand when times were tough
And that's why I love you so much.

Matthew Pickering (13)

Thank You Mums

Thank you mums for everything you gave us!
Thank you mums for the times you spent with us!
Thank you mums for the food and the presents!
Thank you mums for a home and lots of trust!
Thank you mums for everything you do for us!
Thank you mums for your love and care for us!

Aysha Iqbal (11)

My Mum

On the subject of mums,
I think you'll find,
They all tend to be,
Extremely kind.

But I think that mine,
Beats them all,
She's always here,
If I'm upset or fall.

She looks after me,
She's always there,
To cuddle up to,
Like a very soft bear.

To be a top mum,
She's passed the test
And so I must say,
That she's the best.

Freya Chappell (10)

My Mum

She is kind and generous
She always cooks for me
She cares about me
She sometimes cries
She takes me to school
She takes me everywhere
That's my mum.

Gurvinder Bhangal (8)

Mum

I want to say thank you!

Since the day I was able to recognise your voice,
You have always helped me to make the right choice,
All the things you do for my sake,
All the lovely things you make and bake,
All the things you do for me,
You always know how to make me happy,
Making me feel a whole lot better,
Even when the weather seems to be getting wetter,
You've always encouraged me with my dreams,
When you're around, everything beams,
I appreciate everything you do,
Thank you!

Charlie Emsley (13)

My Mum

Everyone says that their mum is the best,
But my mum is better than the rest.

She is like my best friend
And her mad thoughts never end!

She is crazy, kind and loves to shop!
If I didn't have her, my heart would stop!

My mum loves to relax in the sun,
I love her so much, she is so much fun!

My mum means the world to me,
She's always *in* the trend,
My love for her will *never* end!

Ella McEwen (12)

Your Wonderful Mum

She makes your day,
Blows your mind away
From the love she gives to you.

From this you know,
She cares for you head to toe
Never take her for granted.

She would die for you,
No doubt it's true
Why not give something in return?

Without this hero,
You'd really be zero
For she was the one who suffered for you.

From all of your mates,
Even your closest mates
She'll be your best friend ever.

By now you've guessed,
You know she's the best
Your mum needs a rest as well.

So on Sunday,
It will be Mother's Day
And that's your chance to reward her.

Alice Zapparova (12)

A Poem About My Mum

I love my mum
She's such good fun
She works very hard
And gets jobs done!

My mum is so kind
She buys me sweets
And clothes and books
That I like to read!

She's earned a medal
I think she is the best
And on Mother's Day
She deserves a rest!

My mum's so *cool*
I think she is *great*
She's there for me always
And she's my best mate!

Lucy Rolli (11)

I Wonder Why Mothers Are Like Children?

Mums love a little lay-in
They can't get enough of it
I wonder if they are like children
When we're in the classroom and told to sit?

I wonder what mothers are really like
Whether they play
With little kites
And have to have their say?

I wonder
I wonder
If mothers are really like children?

Truth St Louis (10)

My Mum

My mum is very caring and kind,
She's the best mum ever, I think you'll find.
If I'm ill, she'll come running,
Because she's splendid, great and cunning.
She buys me gorgeous and lovely things
And for my birthday she got me a pretty ring.
One of my mum's talents is to bake
And I absolutely love her chocolate cakes.
If it's wet, she picks us up from school,
Then my brother goes outside to play football.
My mum takes us to watch the best new movies,
We say 'Thank you,' and drink our smoothies.
She owns a silver Vauxhall Corsa
And in her kitchen cupboard she has a saucer.
My mum is very good at writing,
But she doesn't really enjoy cycling.
She works in a hospital as a staff nurse,
Which puts money in her purse.
She takes us to places like the safari park,
But not mad things like races with racing karts!
My mum is simply the best,
Certainly better than all the rest.
For world's best mum she won the test,
Because my mum is totally the best.

Laura Edwards (12)

Praise Song For My Mother

You are ...
a tiger to me
protective, strong and brave

You are ...
a lamp to me
guiding me through the darkness

You are ...
a fire to me
warm, bright and comforting

You are ...
an autumn leaf
soft and gentle, falling from the sky
like a gift.

You are ...
Everything to me!

Natalie Howard (14)

Poems For Mum

My mum is the one that knows how to make me smile,
If I'm in an awkward situation then she is always there, ready to give me a hug.
Take a guess who always wins the battle in the sweet aisle.
Mums are the people that you look up to.
My mum can multitask!
She is a good listener and advisor.
Problems with boys are long gone after talking to Mum.
She is a star which shines so brightly that her light nearly blinds me.
I often take fashion tips from her because she always looks so fab!
Shopping is heaven, there is no doubt I'll be bought something new soon.
She spoils me rotten and I love her to bits.
There would be no life for me without Mum.
    Thanks Mum, you're the best!

Lydia Shore (12)

My Mum

My mum is cool
My mum is great
My mum works at school
My mum is never late!

My mum cooks me dinner
My mum helps me with homework
My mum's always a winner
My mum rarely goes berserk!

My mum cleans my clothes
My mum washes the dishes
My mum always sews
My mum gives me lots of kisses!

My mum is cool
My mum is great
My mum works at school
My mum is never late!

Kate Parsons (11)

Thank You

Thank you for all you have done.
You were there for me
And you were the only one,
No matter what it may be.

Thank you for supporting me
When I couldn't do something you gave me the strength,
Then I had the key, I could go to any length.

Thank you for all your great advice
When I was unsure,
My life was like a dice,
I went to you and you had the key to the door.

So thank you Mum.

Kajal Patel (11)

A Thank You To My Mum

Paula Lightfoot

Thank you Mum
For everything you've done,
For everything you've given me
Thank you!

You look after me,
Take care of me,
You're such a dedicated mum
The best mum!

I think you're brilliant,
I don't know how you do it,
But you do, every day.
Don't you?

You cook, you clean,
You're such a great mum.
You're such a cool mum,
But most of all, you're my best friend.

Anna Lightfoot (12)

Thanks Mum

This is a poem for my mum,
I want to say thank you for all that she's done.
She is there for me when others are not,
She's been helping me out since I slept in a cot.
She is always on the move, tidying up,
Cleaning the house and going to the shop.
She will iron my clothes and take me to places,
When I was young she would tie my laces.
She still finds time to read a book
And after that she will go and cook.
She just keeps on going all day long,
She will hardly do anything wrong.
This poem means a great big thanks,
My mum means more to me than all the world's banks.

Paul Aitchison (13)

What My Mam Likes

My mam likes the sun,
When shining so bright.

My mam likes me,
When full of delight.

My mam likes chocolate,
Dark is the best.

My mam likes birds,
Singing in their nest.

My mam likes flowers,
Smelling so sweet.

My mam likes my brother,
He has anything to eat!

She likes our pet Doodle,
Who plays every night.

My mam, my brother and me,
That's the way it should be!

Rachel Star (9)

One Of A Kind

You're one of a kind
And you don't seem to mind,
If I do something wrong, you say,
Try it again, some other day.

You're something special and sacred to me,
A priceless gift from wherever it may be,
I know you've always tried to protect me,
Like I was locked up, and you had the key.

But now I'm a big girl and will soon have to face the world alone,
Getting a job and some day leaving home.
But I'll always love you, it's been fun,
To know you'll be there for me, because you're my mum!

Natalie Elizabeth Steinmetz (12)

The Beautiful Mother

She who stood before me
Dazzling brown eyes
Enticing picturesque skin
A beige, bronze colour
Most beautiful of tans
Wonderfully shaped eyebrows
Like the mountain slopes of Iceland
Black glass strings, shining brightly
For classy hair tied in a collapsing bun
Slender shape
In an old, dull styled dress
Made magnificent by her

And there beside her in handsome blue chariot,
Sat her little prince
He gave a wail
She knelt to comfort him.
Full fuchsia coloured lips pressed together
Humming a gentle lullaby tune
Mauve eyeshadow
Reflecting her gentle comforting eyes,
Portraying: the mother
Untainted
As she should be
The beautiful mother
Her face a mass with piercings and earrings.

Comfort Nwabia (12)

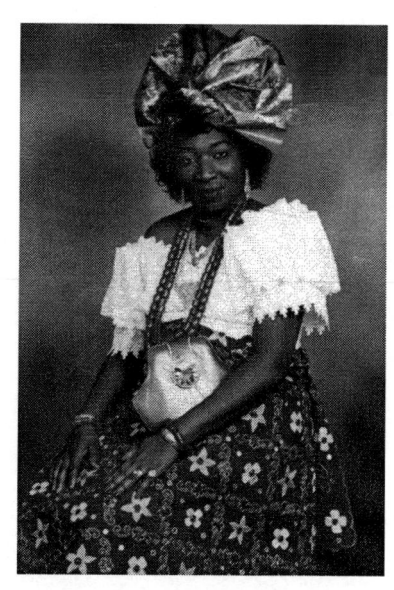

A Poem For My Mum

Washing, cleaning
ironing, cooking
this is what my mum does,
caring, loving
comforting, protecting
this is what my mum does,
my mum's the best
there's no doubt,
I love my mum
all throughout.

Sophie Walters (12)

My Special Someone

She's funny you'll find
She's one of a kind
She takes me to the town
And cheers me up when I'm down
She cleans the house every day
And doesn't let anything get in her way
She looks after me and my brother
Who is this special person you ask?
My special person is my mother.

Nicole Holmes (12)

Always

As the moonlight comes upon me,
My mum is always there,
As the sun rises over the hills,
I know she'll always care.

As the years go by and I get older,
My mum is always there,
As many things as I do wrong,
I know she'll always care.

As my mum is my best friend,
For her, I will be there,
As she brought me into this world,
For her, I will always care.

Cassandra Nelson (13)

My Perfect Mum

With you Mum,
I have a friendship,
I can tell you anything,
Because we share so much love.

We have that mother/daughter bond,
I know I can rely on you,
Our friendship will be forever,
I love you with all my heart.

So that is why I dedicate this poem to you Mum,
Our love and friendship means the world to me,
Your name is so precious,
It will always be engraved in my heart with letters of gold.
I love you!

Katy Furness (13)

My Mother

I'm a lonely child in a dream
And I wait for someone to rescue me
I'm waiting, I'm waiting

In the distance I see a shadow
And I wonder who it is
I wonder, I wonder

The shadow getting nearer
It's now becoming clear
My mother, my mother, she's here.

Katie Lord (12)

My Best Friend

I have a friend who I've known all my life,
She's always there for me when I need advice.

When I was little, if I had a fall,
She'd be there at once, without even a call.

And if I was stuck on a sum or a sheet,
The problem, my friend always helped me to beat.

So now, years later, although I've matured,
She doesn't neglect me nor let me grow bored.

And if there's an issue I'd like to discuss,
We have a good chat and my friend's in no rush.

In the busiest week, on the busiest day,
My best friend, from me, is not far away.

And although we may sometimes shout,
We've never had a big fall-out.

Every month my friend and I go to town,
To look at the clothes and to smile or frown.

We spend many hours deciding on books,
Then share our reviews and try our luck.

So although she's not my only chum,
My very best friend is ...
    My mum!

Tansy B Grady (15)

Thank You Mum

Mum I'd like to thank you,
For standing by me through and through,
You were there when I was first born,
You're always there when I wake in the morn.
My first day at school you helped me then,
You told me what to do and when.
Even though sometimes I am quite mean,
You look after me, you still cook and clean.
When I am hurt you care for me
And you, also, are very good company.
You laugh a lot, you are great fun
And I'll always love you because you're my
Mum!

Laura Caldwell (11)

Mummy

In memory of Janet Cemery, mother of my friend Catherine

Mummy, where are you?
Are you up there above?
In Heaven with God and the angels;
Surrounded by all their love?

Mummy, why did you leave me?
Was it something I've done?
And Mummy, if I said sorry
Would you come back to your son?

Are you an angel now Mummy?
With a dress all sparkly and white?
Do you wear a halo all shimmery, shiny
That comes to brighten my night?

I love you very much Mummy,
I think of you every day
And if you come back to me Mummy,
I'll never go away.

Amy Down (12)

Thank You Mum

My mum will be the nicest person you'd ever meet,
She's always there to lend a hand.
She'd cook my tea
And is always cheering me up.

I'd never know what I'd do without my mom,
She's brought me up with love and respect
And still is now when I'm in my teens,
What would I do without her?

There's just two words I want to say and that's, 'Thank you.'
Thank you for loving me every year of my life,
Spoiling me with gifts and surprises all year through
And feeling glad that I'm your daughter.

So this poem is dedicated to you Mum,
To tell you how grateful and proud I am
Of what you've done for me
And when Mother's Day comes
I'll show you how much I care.

Michelle Bailey (14)

My Mum, Pam

My mum knows everything that mums need to know,
She knows when I need an extra special treat because I'm feeling low,
She knows how to help, whenever I'm stuck,
Whether it's school work or if I've just had a bit of bad luck.
She's always there for me when I've broken up with a friend,
But she knows there's one friend I'll never fall out with,
No matter how much we argue,
No matter how much I put her patience to the test,
My mum knows we'll always be close friends,
Because I know she's the very best!

Radhaika Kumari Kapur (12)

My Mum

Like blooming flowers in a field
Like soft, dewy grass
Like a twitter of a bird
Like all my favourite colours
That's my mum!
Like a butterfly in the sky
Like a warm summer morning
Like a heart made of warmth
Like a rainbow made of smiles
I love you Mum!

Iqra Aslam (11)

My Mum

A smile shines through, day or night,
No matter what grief, or anger, or fright.

The flowers and trees,
The buzz of bees,
Stays by her side,
Always by her side.

There's always a helping hand there,
To make things fair and square,
To cheer me up when I'm down
And look after me, without a frown.

My mum is the best,
She beats the rest,
So thanks for all you've done.

Faye Clayton (11)

Mum

She cooks
She cleans
She loves ducks
And makes me eat my greens.

She's always there wherever I go
She's good at sports
And has a really good throw.

She's funny
She's cool
She won't buy me a bunny
But that's her only rule.

She's the best mum in the world
That's all I can say
She's the best mum in the world
And she's mine, *hooray!*

Alex Drake (11)

No 1 Mum!

No one else can replace my mum
Making homework look quite fun
Always making sure I eat my greens
Keeping the house always clean
Dropping me off at school each day
Helping my dad work every week
Going on holidays around the world
I love my mum who makes my life extremely fun!

Lucy Pullinger (10)

Reason Why Mum Is Special

My mum is someone special who stands right by my side,
My mum is someone who watches out for me when my problems start to collide.
My mum is special because in the morning she has a debate,
Shouting, 'Lauren get up or you'll be late.'
My mum is special because she has two different coloured eyes and long golden hair,
But the best thing of all is she's my mum so there.

Lauren Garbett (10)

And We Always Walk Away Without A Word

Mum, you are always there,
Through the good times and the bad,
You buy us the best clothes and toys,
When we have problems you sort them,
And we always walk away without a word.

Mum, you hold our hand,
To make sure we are safe,
You detest to see us hurt,
You are always there to help,
And we always walk away without a word.

Mum, you never give up on us,
Whether we be good or bad,
And I don't think you ever will,
You are the best mum we could have,
And we always walk away without a word.

Mum, why do you get cross?
Is it because you want us to learn?
Do you need us like we need you?
Could this possibly be true?
And we always walk away without a word.

Mum, you have been an angel to us all,
Without you we wouldn't have coped,
Although we are bigger, we still need you,
And we have two little words to say,
Thank you.

Michael Johnston (15)

Instructions For Growing A Perfect Mum

You start with the heart
And put it in a special spot,
The base is care
And you need quite a lot.

Then add a sprinkle of anger,
As she has to be fairly strict,
topped with a thick layer of love
And a sweet smell, freshly picked.

Also a shovelful of respect
And some smartness too,
Don't forget to add energy,
As she has a lot to do.

After you've added all the nutrients,
Then you've finished planting your mum,
Just make sure she stays happy while growing
And your perfect mum will soon come.

And when she comes she'll care for you and love you,
Be there when you are sad,
There when you need help,
She'll be the best thing you've ever had.

I hope you love your mum
And treasure her every day,
Appreciate everything she does for you
And love her in every single way!

Jodie O'Donnell (14)

A Poem For My Mum

You must have been brilliant
At school in classes, Sandy
Painting away in art, but at break
Offering everyone candy

The thing people would like
Is you really smile a lot
And when people give you presents
You hug them with all you've got

The embarrassing thing about you, Mum
Is you make me look a jerk
The good thing about you though
Is that you do all the work!

Natalie Robson (11)

It's All About Love

Hey Mum I'd just like to say
I'll always love you in every way.
You're kind and gentle, you make me feel warm
And that's how I've felt ever since I was born.

Every mum gets angry in a way
And says things that they don't mean to say,
But I've always found it in my heart
To forgive you right from the very start.

When I get angry I get really mad
Then I say things that are horrible and bad.
When I say things they may sound true,
But honestly I don't mean to hurt you.

So Mum I meant what I said from the start
And I know that you've got it inside your heart,
So what I mean and am writing above,
Is I'm trying to say that we've got the love.

Kirsty Rollason (14)

Beautiful

M y mum is the best
O ther mums aren't as good as my mum
T he sun only shines when my mum smiles
H er hair shines like the moon on a lake
E lizabeth is her name
R oses are her favourite but she is my number one rose.

Joshua Everett (10)

My Mum!

My mum is really special,
I love her very much,
She always cooks good food for me,
That I really really love.
When she's sad, I make her happy,
But when she's angry, I say sorry.
She sometimes buys me gifts,
When I'm doing my homework very well.
She is my best mum in the world!
I love my mum.

Josephine Goh (9)

Motherly Love

It's the 22nd
And you'd just given birth,
A pretty girl I was,
But purple at first.
You took me in your arms
And cuddled me tight and close,
To everyone that came to see me,
All you did was boast.
You took me to school
And waited by my side,
When I got stuck on my work,
Your love was my guide.
It's 15 years later
And you're still here for me,
Wherever I need you,
There you'll always be.
You taught me many things,
Read, write and love,
They say I was a gift,
But it's you who's sent from above.

Leonie Reed (15)

My Mum

She's not just a mum to me,
She's a mum to all us three,
Sister, brother and me,
Breakfast, dinner and tea,
Washing, ironing, cleaning,
My mum does everything for me.
Most of the time I am good,
But sometimes I may be bad,
That's when Mum shouts Dad!
Without my mum I would be sad,
So to have her I am so glad.
I love my mum now and forever
And hope we will always be together.

Chelsea Butler (8)

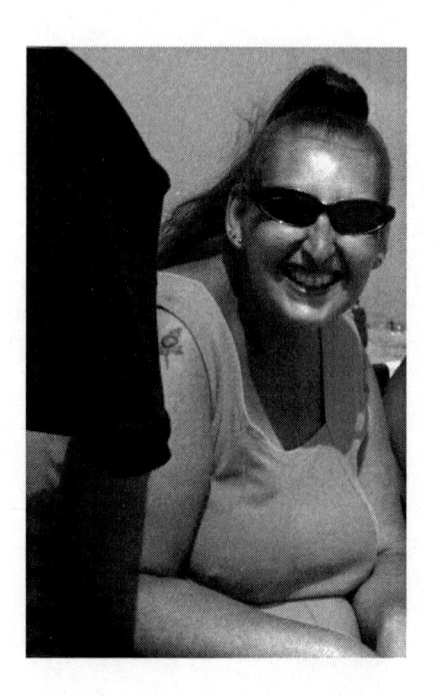

To My Mum

Like a dream, you fill my head,
even when I'm not in bed.
Your eyes that sparkle like polished gold,
a sign of the trust we'll always hold.
Birds sing happy, high in the trees
and your lustrous hair wafts in the breeze.
Your laugh is like a summer's day,
that makes me wish you'll never go away.
Your smile, it lights a darkening night
and it fills my heart, which soars like a kite
And your radiant heart is overflowing with love,
which makes me believe you were born up above.
You cheer me up when I am glum,
a shining star, you are my mum!

Hannah Bolt (14)

Mum You're The Best

Mum this poem is just for you,
For all the special things you do,
You're my very best friend,
My love for you will never end,
All the rough times you've pulled me through,
That great quality I learnt from you,
You've always helped me with my troubles,
Some people say we are doubles,
Well what more can I say?
My trust for you grows each day,
You're the person I want to be when I'm older,
So instead you can cry on my shoulder,
I hope this poem has made you see,
How much you really mean to me.

Sammi-Jo Ward (12)

Happy Mother's Day!

Mum, thank you,
Mum, hope you
Have a great day
Because today
Is Mother's Day!

So you have a rest
While I bake something
You like best!

Amun Bal (11)

My Mum

I love my mum
The way she is
Not a film star
Or in showbiz

She buys me sweets
She cooks me tea
And she is always
There for me

I love my mum
For the things she does
Making me feel special
She's my one true love.

Rosie Grieve (9)

My Mum

My mum is so great,
She's one of the best,
She's no one to hate,
She's better than the rest.

She takes you on trips
And on vacations,
She helps you so much,
In sticky situations.

She helps you with homework
And things you can't do.
She cooks and she cleans
And walks the dog too!

There is one reason,
Why my mum needs flowers.
She works and she works
Day and night - all hours!

Rachel Stanley (11)

Cool Mum

My mum is great,
She scrapes the plates
And she cleans the floor,
Makes the tea for half-past four,
My mum is great.

She has ginger hair
And looks like Fozzie Bear,
I love my mum,
She likes her soaps,
Sat with butter and toast,
But most of all I love my mum the most.
I love you Mum.

Sarah Jane Simpson (16)

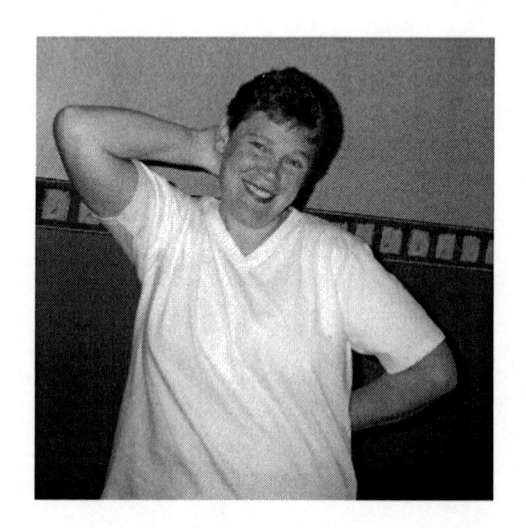

My Mum

My mum's like the sea,
She is really full of glee
She likes to have a rest
Watching the musical 'Chess'.

She likes to read books,
Scrumptious cakes she cooks.
She takes us to shows,
Songs and plays she knows.

She makes history fun,
Her face lights up like the sun.
She isn't ever dumb,
That's my super mum.

Clare Stevens (10)

My Mum

My mum is the best
She's always better than the rest
She'd do anything for me
And she doesn't have a fee

Whenever I need her, she's always there
Ready to share, love and care
I really couldn't ask for a better mum than you
That's because you love me and I love you too.

Jess Teggart (13)

Mum

When I am down
She'll bring me back up
And when we go to town
She'll buy me things that I adore

When I am sad
She gives me a shoulder to cry on
And when things are bad
She'll be there to put it right

When it turns night
And I get scared
My mum gets the light
And now I'm alright

My mum is my best friend
My mum will be there until the end.

Cindel Simmill (14)

I Love My Mum

My mum is fun,
My mum is cool,
My mum sometimes acts the fool
She dances about, laughs and jokes,
She dresses up in silly coats.
There is always time for love and kisses,
Even when she's washing dishes.
She cooks my tea and cleans my clothes,
But there's one thing she always knows,
I love my mum!

Chloe Schofield (9)

Mum And Me

I love my mum
She loves me too
There's lots of things that we two do
We sit and talk
She reads me books
We also share great big hugs
I love my mum
She's sweet and kind
I'd like to think she's all mine.

Katie Schofield (9)

My Mum

My mum she always looks pretty, nice, long, curly hair
And her beautiful clothes.
My mum cooks my lovely tea
And makes my lunch for my lunch box.
She's the only one who could have me born ...
So just before you open your mouth
And say a lot of nasty words to your mum,
Just think about all the things she does for you.

Jonathan Venus (9)

Mum The Chatterbox

Chatter, chatter, chatter at the bus stop and school front door,
I can't take it anymore.
Chatter in the village,
Chatter in the street,
'Come on,' I say, 'I want my treats.'
Chatter on the phone,
Chatter at the store,
Come on Mum I can't wait anymore.
My mum's friends are just as bad,
Are all grown-ups chatter mad?
I may sound a little cross,
But I love my mum, the chatterbox.

Rosanna Bucknill (10)

My Fantastic Mum

In the misty mornings I cannot see, but this person would see.
This person is great, she is strong and tough.
This person is good enough for me!

This person is fantastic, she is funny,
When she dances and sings.
This person is kind and helpful!

This person does not need anybody to fight her battles,
Because she can handle it herself.
That's why I love this person very much.

Who is this person?
This person is my *mum!*

Abbie Mitchell (11)

POEMS FOR MUM 2006 EDITION

My Mum!

My mum is the nicest mum there is around,
She makes me breakfast,
She darns my socks, she irons my T-shirts,
She always is there for my sister and me
And not forgetting my dad!
She makes me smile, she makes me laugh,
She makes me crazy when she sings 'The Sound of Music',
But the best thing about Mum is she's the family's ...
Own personal *chauffeur!*

Charlotte Morris (13)

My Mum

As I wake up from my delightful dream,
I see a beautiful face shining like a sunray's beam.

>She has eyes of river blue,
>With an angel's voice that comforts you.

A smell of crispy bacon and scrumptious eggs floats through,
As she says, 'I've made a cooked breakfast - just for you.'

>Parma Violets perfumes,
>When I'm around her looms,

It teases my nose,
Like a cricket on a restful rose.

>As I give her a kindly cuddle,
>She feels like a cashmere bundle,

Of lots of joy, memories of gold
And advice I am told.

>Sunday is her special day,
>In a very special way,

She cooks a radiant roast,
(Something in which I can boast!)

>with brilliant broccoli and perfect potatoes,
>it wisps away any feeling of woe,

and afterwards a cake,
that no one else will ever be able to make.

>This person is ...
>My mum.

Daisy Maria Harvey (11)

I Love My Mum

I love my mum,
She's the best,
Even though she makes me wear a vest!

I love my mum,
She's kind of cool,
Even when she skateboards to school!

I love my mum,
She's kind of sweet
And always buys me lots of treats!

I love my mum,
For everything,
Even though she cannot sing!

I love my mum,
But most of all,
I'm glad she's my mum
And I'm not too tall!

I love my mum because she's gentle
And I know I drive her mental!
I love my mum,
You're the best,
But please don't make me wear a vest!

Rebecca Parker (9)

I Need You Mum!

I need you Mum, I love you
If you weren't there what would I do?
I need you Mum to give me some help
If you weren't who would have dealt?
I need you Mum, without you I wouldn't dare
If you weren't there who would care?

Punika Kotecha (10)

Superwoman

Worklady/housewife
No good at baking cakes
Never, ever comes on time
But non-stop from the moment she wakes.

Always dead professional
And *always* takes care
Washing, ironing and cleaning
It just never seems fair.

Cleaning is not her hobby
And dusting - not on the list
Doing a million things at once
She needs to turn and twist.

So calling on all housewives
I'm the next of kin
Well then let's make an announcement
Mum you're a superwoman.

Samantha Croal (12)

My Mother!

My mother is so lovely,
My mother is so kind.

Whenever I have a problem,
She is always there for me.

My mother picks me up when I fall,
She is like my best friend.

My mother takes great care
Of me and my brothers.

My mother is the best mother
You can ever imagine.

Deva Edwards (12)

My Mum

Mum,
You are always there,
Thanks for the everlasting care.
You are always cheerful,
Always smily,
Never sad,
Never whiny.

Mum,
You help me out,
You are never in doubt,
Your constant guiding,
Keeps me smiling,
Rain or shine,
You're forever mine.

Rebecca Oborne (13)

Mum

She's more than just a doormat
An extra special mate
She's someone to rely on
'Cause she's never ever late.

And when you're feeling needy
When you're feeling blue
She's always there by your side
To care and comfort you

Some people might say weird
others could say sad
But my best friend is always there
She's married to my dad

She's perfect in almost every way
She loves me more than some
You might know who this person is ...
You are *great!*
Thanks Mum.

Phoebe Wall (11)

Best Mum

My mum is always there,
Taking me everywhere.
She makes me happy,
When I'm sad.
She helps me when I'm stuck,
But the best thing about her is
She's kind, helpful, caring and the best.

Rebekah Fenwick (10)

Mum

Mum
Mother
Ma.
Whatever the name,
I wouldn't go far
To slander, to sneer,
To make you sound queer.
Ma
Mother
Mum.
Whatever I call you,
I'll always come
When my name you call,
(Unless I can't hear 'cause I'm in the hall)
Ma
Mum
Mother.
Whatever it is,
I wouldn't want another,
I'm happy with *you* as my mother.

Katy Morgan (11)

Mum Is...

Mum is a fuchsia, swaying in the sun,
Mum is that home-baked smell,
As she hands me a bun.

Mum is that strained smile,
As she sets off to school or Brownies,
Mum is that shake of the head,
As she tries to resist a tube of Rowntrees.

Mum is that little oval pair of specs,
Which she uses to drive the car,
Mum is the sneaker, of my lunch box cake bar.

Mum is the tidier, of under the bed and on the floor,
But the one bad thing about my mum
Is that she calls me Eleanor!

Ellie McIntyre (10)

My Mum

I love my mum,
She always fills my tum.
She loves me,
She always cooks my tea.

She is always there,
She always cares.
If I feel sad,
She never makes me feel bad.

She is the best,
Even when I'm a pest.
She knows everything,
Happiness she'll bring.

She's my favourite person worldwide,
She loves me, even though I have lied.
She likes a glass of wine,
She is mine!

In the day she has fun,
Her party has just begun.
It's nearly her special day, hip hip hooray!

She enjoys going out,
She's always out and about.
I love my mum, she's not dumb.

I love her with all my heart,
Except one little part
And she loves me
And that's the end of my story!

Victoria Rostock (13)

My Mum

My mum is beautiful in every single way,
My mum is beautiful every single day.
My mum loves me lots and lots and lots,
My mum even loved me when I had chickenpox.
My mum is great, hip hip hooray,
My mum is perfect and I love her every day.

Sam Martin Watts (9)

When I Spoil My Mum

My mum always spoils me.
But on Mother's Day it's different,
It's my turn to spoil her.
I would take her breakfast in bed!
Then when she finished her breakfast
I would give her one very special card,
A present and a big bunch of flowers.

When she had opened all her pressies
I would take the dirty plates to the kitchen and wash up.
(It's funny I don't usually do the washing up!)

Whilst Mum would put her feet up,
Watching her favourite soap, 'EastEnders',
I would be doing all the chores, polishing, hoovering,
Wash the dog and feed the cats
And everything else you could think of.

And when it came to the end of the day (yes finally!)
Mum thanked me by saying, 'Today was bliss,
Could you please arrange for every day to be like this?'

Happy Mother's Day Mum. Love you lots like Jelly Tots.
Lots of love Mel x.

Melanie Rayner (12)

Mum

I used to look at her
Like she was made to do
The cooking, the cleaning
And a million other things too.
But now that I'm older
I look with new eyes
At her rushing around
And realise
That she cooks and she cleans
And does more than she should
But we take her for granted
And that's not good.
I should appreciate
What she does for me
She tidies our home and she cooks our tea.
And also with four kids
To watch over each day
She would bend over backwards
To know we were OK.
So thanks to all mums
Who are out there today
And I suppose that is all
That I wanted to say.

Vicky Adelmant (11)

My Mum

My mum,
Her love and devotion,
Her soft gentle touch,
The reassuring look in her eye,
The warm embrace when she hugs me,
My mum.

My mum,
Her favourite TV programme whispers in the background,
Her latest joke about to be told,
The cake that she makes when I come home from camp,
The sweet scent of perfume on her clothes,
My mum.

My mum,
The look in her eye when I know I'm in trouble,
Her whispering voice as she passes on her knowledge and wisdom,
Her cheerful laugh as I crack a joke,
The feeling of everlasting love,
My mum.

Helena Eccles (11)

My Unsung Heroine!

She does up my laces
And pulls funny faces
And cheers when I come last in sports day races.

She waits at the gate,
Tries not to be late,
She knows what I like, she knows what I hate.

She held my hand tight,
Prayed I should fight,
She sat at the hospital bed through the night.

She read me Aesop's fables
And taught me my tables,
She's sown on at least a thousand name labels.

She hides the tears
And all the fears,
As I talk about exciting careers.

For me she'd walk a thousand miles,
She's always ready with loving smiles,
She sees me through the daily trials.

She calls me her little flower
And from her I'll never cower,
And for kisses, well I get a shower.

She can bake a scone,
But not sing a song,
My ears are still ringing from the last time she's singing.

She looks over me every hour,
Her love is like a big strong tower,
I feel the love, I feel the power.

Even though we sometimes fight
Our disagreements are only slight,
Forgiveness and love are always in sight.

Eleanor Easton (11)

Untitled

The best person in my life is my stepmum
I can always talk to her
Any problems I have in life
I know I can always share
Short blonde hair and bright green eyes
She is trendy,
She's too lazy to go shopping for me
But I get to make my own choices
She makes me independent
Thank you for these seven years
The best mum ever, Eva.

Gemma Altham (13)

A Poem For Mum

My mum is kind, gentle and loving
She's always there for you
Even if you're hurt too.
She helps you if you're stuck with something
She helped you come into the world
And teaches you manners so you're not rude.
She gave me a lovely name
And teaches me some fun games.
She tucks me up in my bed
And gives me a kiss on the head.
My mum is the best
Better than the rest.
She feeds me and buys me clothes
And helps me when I paint my toes
I love my mum.

Nicole Petrillo (12)

Fab Mum

My mum's fantastic
Man she's clever and so artistic
She can mend anything
She can tell extravagant jokes
Cares about old folks
Can't beat her one on one with gardening
But she ain't so good
She can make gangster food
Never was she good at swimming
But can do good skimming
She can knit
Knits so many mitts
They say she's no good
Cos she's so hood
It's fine to have a mum like mine.

Jigar Patel (13)

Dear Mam

All through the drama
I can always depend on ma mam
And when it seems that I'm hopeless
You say the words that get me back in focus
When I was sick as a little kid
To keep me happy there's no limit to the things you did
And all my childhood memories
Are full of all the sweet things you did for me
And even though I ain't crazy
I gotta thank the Lord that you made me
There are no words to express how I feel
You never kept secrets, always stayed real
And I appreciate how you raised me
And all the extra love that you gave me
I wish I could take the pain away
If you can make it through tonight
There's a brighter day
Everything will be alright if you hold on
It's a struggle every day gotta roll on
And there's no way I can pay you back
But my plan is to show that I understand.
You are appreciated.

Jessica Copland (14)

A Cherished Mother

Mum you are so special
because you've got me
You brought me into this world
And you've loved me since I was wee

Since I'm growing up so fast
I'd like to give you something that will last
A great big kiss and a lovely hug
And as always all my love.

Mica Sinforiani (11)

Mums

Mums are special
Mums are sweet
Mums are really a special treat.

I buy her chocolate
I buy her flowers
But money can't buy anything
The love she gives me all day and all hours.

I love my mum very much
But I can't repay the amount of love
She gives me every day.

Katherine Hill (12)

Mumsy

My mumsy thinks she's clumsy,
but she's really as nimble as a kite.

My mumsy thinks she's clumsy,
but really she's as hot as a bun ...

Even though my mum is pretty,
she doesn't want a cute wee kitty,
she would prefer a JCB,
(that's much cooler if you ask me!)

My mumsy does not wear a dress,
she comes to breakfast in a mess,
that does not make me love her less.

My mumsy is so very fast,
in a race she'd never be last.

My mumsy is so very fun,
she looks on me as her 'little hun'!

My mumsy may be quite tough,
she may look a little rough,
this does not make me love her less,
she's still my mum,
to her, 'God bless!'

Emma Atkinson (12)

POEMS FOR MUM 2006 EDITION

My Mum

My mum says that she works hard,
But I don't agree!
So after all,
What does she do all day?
When I'm at school
Working hard?

She goes to work she says,
Testing people's eyes.
It can't be that hard,
Can it? After all,
She still has plenty of time,
To look after my brother, Dad and me!

Helping with homework,
Decorating and DIY.
Cooking, cleaning, ironing
And even gardening too.
Ferrying me here and there,
Now what else does she do?

She takes me shopping,
Horse riding too.
We go cycling and swimming together.

How can she say that she's old?
She certainly doesn't act it to me!

My mum, my best friend!

Catrin Davies (11)

My Mum

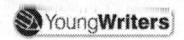

My mum is the best
Better than all the rest
She does the cleaning
Day in day out
She protects me wherever I go
She's always there to listen
Even when there is a problem
She helps to sort it out
She carts me around
When I need a lift
As that's what mums are for
Even though they have a life of their own
Takes me to school
Helps with homework
Tells me I watch too much TV
More exercise will do me good
Treats me kindly and *with love*
Even when I'm naughty
She will understand
That's why mums are here to love.

Louise Balloch (11)

My Mum's The One

I wouldn't be anywhere without my mum,
My mum's a hero, my mum's the one.

> She is the reason why I'm here
> And was the one who called me dear.

>> She is the one who tucked me up
>> And fed me from my first cup.

> She is the one who held me tight,
> When I was scared, frightened at night.

She feeds me always night and day
And keeps my sad tears at bay.

> She is the one who washes my clothes,
> And rubs clear my runny nose.

>> She helps when I can't do work,
>> Even when she is overworked.

> She earns us money so we can live
> And almost always forgives.

She is the one who I love
And calls me her own little dove.

> I wouldn't be anywhere without my mum,
> My mum's a hero, my mum's the one.

Erin Considine (11)

My Mummy Had A Bump

My mummy had a bump
Like a small heffalump
Right on her tummy
My poor mummy

One day it was gone
Surprised was none
Nope, not nobody
Except me!

Nobody told me
What to expect
And the biggest shock of all
Came next day

It was horrible!
A nasty noise and a smell
My parents were distracted
- I could tell

All around me
It was all changing
New people
New places

Instead of my fun space
I found a no go space
My cars and my train set
Became dollies and Tweenies

And in the porch
Where my bike used to stay
Now stands a pram
Not much fun to play!

Why was Mummy ignoring me?
Did I do anything wrong?
My daddy was not there
It had been going on for too long

I asked my teacher
About the horrible creature
And she replied
'It's a baby! Your mummy must be busy!'

When I got home however
My mummy was asleep
The baby was crying
It's been like this all week

I want to help my mummy
But when I try
I get told off
I only want to help!

And then the day came
When my mum sat me down
And making sure
That no one else was around

She told me that she loved me
That she didn't want me to cry
So she took me out instead
For a beef and onion pie

We sat there in the fish shop
For hours on end
She explained about the baby
And how her love could never end

She didn't mean to be horrible
She didn't want to hurt
She was just very busy
Trying to make things work

My mummy did have a bump
Very much like a heffalump
And it was on the tummy
Of my lovely mummy

One day it was gone
Surprised was none
Because my sister
My best friend

Was born!

Alicja Borsberry-Woods (11)

A Poem On Mums

Mums are wicked
Mums are great
And when you most need them
They're your mate!

They make you laugh
They make you cry
But somehow I just
Don't know why!

Some can be good
Some can be bad
But some can make their children
Very, very sad!

Some work through
Twenty-four seven
But now we have to help
Because we're 11!

Some are big
Some are small
But it doesn't matter
Because we love them all!

Jessica Bennett (11)

My Mum's Better Than Yours!

My mum's better than yours
my mum is,
My mum can run faster
my mum can.

My mum's nicer than yours
my mum is,
My mum cuddles me
my mum does.

My mum's the best
my mum is,
My mum won a competition
my mum did.

My mum's clever
my mum is,
My mum can count to 100
my mum can.

My mum's prettier than yours
my mum is,
My mum says I'm pretty
my mum does.

My mum cooks
my mum does,
My mum's the best cook
my mum is.

My mum loves me
my mum does,
Your mum doesn't
my mum *does!*

Ashley Dodds (11)

The Wonderful Thing About Mothers

Based on 'The Tigger Song'

The wonderful thing about mothers,
Is mothers are wonderful things.
They're so much better than brothers,
I should know I've got two of the things.

The things my mother does for me,
She makes my breakfast, cooks my tea,
Washes my clothes, buys me shoes,
Helps me find the things I lose.

I ought to list what I do for Mum,
But what's there to write? Well ... um.
I know she means the world to me
And try to make her pots of tea.

Mums are great, mums are good,
They help you do the things you should.
They teach you to know right from wrong,
Sit up when you're sick the whole night long.

But

They don't wash your clothes for when you need them,
Then tidy your room so you can't find anything.
They tease you when your mates are round
And tell their own friends I'll be bound!

To leave this on a happy note mums are great
They're cuddly cuddly
Cuddly cuddly
Fun
Fun
Fun
Fun
Fun
But the most wonderful thing about mothers ...
... At least I've only one!

Margaret Coleman (11)

Mums

My mum is the best
And so say all the rest,
Mums do most of the work,
Mums clean up all the dirt,
Mums give birth to us,
Mums look after us.

My grannie brought up my mum,
My grandma's 91,
My grannie's got grey hair,
My grandma is the mother of my dad,
This year was my grannie's 50th wedding anniversary,
My grandma's 65th.

Of great grans I had four,
But I can only remember one,
She was old with white hair,
She smelt of cologne,
She had to have a wheelchair to go out,
She was scarred by two wars.

When I grow up I may become a mother,
To some children of my own,
But now my mum is doing work
And my grans are probably too,
My family tree shows lots of people,
But I am at the bottom.

Clare Carr (11)

My Mum

She's always there
Waiting at the gate
With her dazzling smile
She's never late.

Once we're home
She gets me tea
Sometimes McDonald's
Or KFC!

She'll look at my homework
Maths and art
She can do them all
And helps me start.

Later that night
She runs me a bath
We overflow it with bubbles
And make each other laugh.

When it's time for bed
In she'll come
I'll give her a hug
And say 'I love you Mum!'

Suzy Davenport (12)

Mums

Some mums are fun,
most of the time,
Some mums are loving,
especially mine.

Some mums are cool,
even when your friends are round.
Some mums are quiet,
and don't make a sound.

Some mums are loud
and dance around.
Some mums are lively
and hardly touch the ground.

Some mums are clever
and get everything right.
Some mums have jobs,
even at night.

Some mums are different,
but are still special.
Some mums are great
and are wonderful mates.

Bethan Dalby (11)

My Mum, Thank You

Thank you for my mum
Thank you for everything you do for me
Thank you for my bed you make
Thank you for washing the pots
Thank you for the clothes you wash.

Regan Everson (10)

Thanks Mum

Thank you Mum for everything,
Thank you Mum for the toys you bring.
Thanks for the lovely cheese whirls
And for having one girl.
Thank you for being beautiful,
One more thing,
Tidy my room!

Niall Cullen (10) & Declan Hirrell (7)

Untitled

Thank you Mum for all the food you buy for us,
If it wasn't for you we would have no food in the cupboard.
Thank you for look after us and thank you for loving us too
But the best thing in life is you Mum.
I love you Mum.

Anthony Thomas

Thank You Mum

Thank you Mum for being yourself,
And for cleaning my room.

Thank you Mum for cooking our food,
And for taking me to school.
You're the best mum I could have.

Chelsea Hill (11)

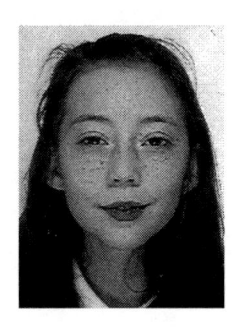

Thank You Mum

Thank you for the food I eat
Thank you for the growing wheat
Thank you for always understanding me
Thank you for letting me sit on your knee
Thank you for giving me shelter
Thank you from stopping me welter.
One thing I have to say Mum is, 'Thank you!'

Tayla Houston (10)

My Mum Is The Best

I thank my mum for gifts I get
And also for the food she puts on my plate
And the clothes I get.

Thank you for being with me
And thank you for being helpful to me.

Courtney Wallace (10)

Thank You Mummy

Thank you Mummy,
I thank you a lot.
You feed my tummy
With chicken broth pot.
I think you're so cool
Because you take me to the swimming pool.
You give me a shelter
And clothes to wear.
You cool me down when I welter
And buy me little teddy bears.
Thank you for being funny
And most of all thank you for being my mummy.

Jade Evans (10)

Thank You Mum

Thank you for the clothes you buy,
Thank you for the help you give me,
Thank you for the fun you give to me,
Thank you for the toys you give me.

Katie Heapy (10)

My Mum

I thank my mum for loving me.
I thank my mum for my food.
I thank my mum for my clothes.
My mum is so cool.

Craig Kinsella (10)

Mum!

Thank you Mum for always being there for me,
Always willing to help
And you're always cracking me up when I'm feeling down.
I love it when you come to me and hug me tight,
Just like a Christmas present.
I don't know what I would do without you
And you're always lighting up my world.
I promise Mum I will never forget you.

Liam Carpenter (9)

Mum

Mum, you look like a star shining above the world,
Your dress is pretty and you look like a buttercup
Getting prettier and prettier every day.
I love you because you're bright.
I love you day and night.
I hug you in bed still smelling the nature.
Your hug is warm with a dressing gown on,
You are kind to me, you make my heart stronger.
Mum you are so lovely, I can't live without you.
I love you Mum!
Love from Jazzmin.

Jazzmin Robinson (10)

Mum

Mum, as I think of you, my face lights up and smiles,
You are as pretty as a princess.
The world doesn't know how special mums are.
You wrap me up with your arms,
I feel like a birthday present with a scarf,
You are always there and I cannot say you aren't.
You are my best friend and it will never end.
See you soon, love you loads, love from your one and only.

Liberty Edler Davies (10)

Mum's The Word

Thank you Mum you are the best,
Better than all the rest.
I love you with all my heart,
I couldn't live without you, even with Dad.
Mum your heart glows like gold,
Each day I wait for a hug when you enter the door,
You work all day to keep us happy.
Mum you're the best and I'll always remember you.
Love from Billy.

Billy Elsey (9)

Mum

Thank you Mum, you are the best.
Could not live without you,
Just can't wait to get my hug.
Mum you shine like the stars and the big yellow sun.
Mum your heart glows like gold.
I've made my point, that you are the best!
I just want to say,
Thank you, love from Danny!

Danny Dabin (9)

Mum

Thank you Mum for everything you do,
You light up my day like a golden rainbow shining down,
You are as busy as a bumblebee and you're always there for me,
You always come and tuck me in,
I love you from the bottom of my heart,
You're the best in the world and I will always love you.

Joshua White (9)

Mummy, Yummy!

Pretty as a rose, I love you, you treasure,
Having you for a mum, it's a dear, dear pleasure.
Sweet as a bunny, guess who? that's you!
You cute, cute, cute, sweet, sweet, sweet
Pretty, pretty, pretty, Mummy Bunny!

Rosy cheeks, brunette hair, you're as fluffy as a bear!
Lovely, considerate, kind and sweet,
Lots of your home-made buns to eat!

Carly Stone (9)

Mum

Mum, you are the best and I love you with all my heart,
You're always there if I need you!
Your smile warms me up every day
However I'm glad to be your child.
You grow prettier every day, as time goes past!
I think you're the voice of nature guiding me towards the Earth and stars.
You are like the cherry on top of a cake.
You tuck me in every night until I go to sleep.
Mum, Mum remember I love you.

Amelia Clark (9)

I Love My Mum

Mum you are the best,
You're better than the rest.
I love you truly with my heart,
Mum you are the best.
You buy me this, you buy me that.
I'll never forget you,
Mum you are the best.
I'm grateful for the things you do,
Mum you are the best.
Our love will never ever change,
Mum you are the best.
I think you now need to know
That Daddy made the right choice to marry you
And love you lots.
You really are the best.

Hannah Lee (9)

My Mummy Is The Best

I love you Mummy, *kiss! Kiss! Kiss!*
I bet you will thank me just for this.

I will love you with all my heart
You are always there, right at the start.

I love you loads no matter what
You're not a bee I would swat!

Sometimes you lose the plot
But who cares, I do not!

Every time I have a hug
I feel warm, happy and snug.

When I go to my bed
I would rather a kiss instead!

Thanks Mum!

Charlotte Wakefield (9)

My Mummy Is The Best

Kiss, kiss, kiss,
I bet you will thank me just for this,
I love you loads, no matter what,
You're not the bee that I would swat.
Sometimes you lose the plot, but who cares?
I do not!
I want to say, 'You're the best.'
To have you as a mum, I feel blessed.
I'll never forget you throughout my life.
So thank you!

April Walker

A Poem For You, Mum

Mum, you're always there for me,
You light up my life.
You always care for me in a loving way.
You are my best friend and always will be.
To tell you the truth, I could never live without you.
So mum, I know you get mad but deep in your heart you
Will always love me like I love you!
From your darling Abigail xxx

Abigail Goodwin (9)

A Poem For My Mum

Mum, you'll always be in my heart,
Whenever you tuck me in at night,
I can never wait to see you tomorrow.
I'll tell you the truth,
I could never live without you.
Mum, you will always lighten up my world.

Love from Libby xxx

Libby Smith

My Marvellous Mum

Mum, you are the best anyone could meet,
You're always by my side.
Even when you shout, I will always love you
Throughout my heart.
You are as beautiful as a princess,
I'm always thinking of you wherever I go,
But there's something you need to know.
I really, truly love you forever.

Tyler Barrow (9)

Mum

Mum, you are the best and I will love you forever,
You are the best mum ever.
You are as warm as the sun,
Thank you for looking after me,
You are the sun shining in my world,
Mum, you are the best and I will always love you.

James Kose (9)

A Message To My Mum

Mum you're as sweet as a rose, you're as fast as a cheetah,
You're as busy as a bumblebee and as caring as a mummy lion cuddling her cub.
You look after me even if I'm unwell or sad.
You're my best friend in the whole wide world.
I'll never forget you and all the things
You have done for me.

Danny O'Halloran (9)

The Mother's Poem

You're as sweet as a rose and as shiny as a rainbow,
And you will always light up my heart like a golden rainbow, shining down.
Your eyes lighten up the house, like the sun itself.
And your smile is as big as a clown's.

Harry Webster (9)

Mummy You're Lovely

Mum, you wrap me up nice and tight,
you're there, day and night.

You shine in my dreams to make
them fine.

You're as busy as a bee, you're as
precious as a treasure.
I'll take good care of your forever.

You and only you will be there,
you are the very best I can ever have.

Happy Mother's Day.

Lara Leyser (9)

It Is All About You, Mum

Thank you for holding me tight every night,
Thank you for giving me a warm home to rest in.
Thank you for giving me a different lifestyle.
Thank you for helping me up when I fall over.
Thank you for being the best mum ever.

Ryan Simmons (10)

Mum

Mum, I love your bright face,
I love you so much, you would not be able
to think of the number.
But Mum, you are as beautiful as the sun.
You cannot dream of how much I love you.

Charlie-Boy Howard

My Beloved Mother

In loving memory of Debbie Ellis

I close my eyes and a tear brushes down my cheek,
I place the flowers down in the graveyard, so bleak.
Maybe one day I can tell you what I want to say,
You've passed away but in my heart you will always stay,
I love you and I always will,
Time seems to have stopped, completely still,
I miss your smiley face,
And how you always brightened up the place.
I miss every little tiny thing,
I even miss how you used to always sing,
I want to thank you for everything,
You were my mum, nothing will change it, not anything,
Everything seemed so perfect and fine,
You were our mum, my sister and mine!

Dawn Ellis (14)

My Mummy

My mummy's very friendly
My mummy's very fair
My mummy's very happy
My mummy's got brown hair

My mummy's very kind
And my mummy isn't vile
My mummy's very cheery
My mummy wears a smile

My mummy's very organised
My mummy's very calm
My mummy's got blue eyes
I'm like her little lamb

When I'm in a situation
Where I don't know where to stand
Then my mummy's always there
To give me that helping hand

When I feel really sad
Or my brother is a pest
Or when the teacher's screaming
I like my mummy best.

Thomas Bartos (9)

My Helpful Mum

Mum I love you because
You are beautiful like a rose.
You are very hard-working,
You are very humorous, like a comedian
You are polite, like a daisy.

Mum, I love you because
You are as gentle as a butterfly.
You are so generous
You are loving and caring.
You are a smashing mother.

Mum, I love you because
You are warm-hearted, like a big heart,
You are so sweet to me
You are so special to me, that's why I love you.

Elizabeth Ashamu (8)

My Helpful Mum

Mum, I love you because you are beautiful
like a red rose
You are funny when you tell me jokes
You are the greatest mum in the world

Mum I love you because you are beautiful
and caring like a rainbow
You buy me lots of clothes
You wake me up in the morning
You are so helpful

Mum I love you because when I'm sad
you cheer me up
When I'm naughty you don't get angry
I'm writing this poem to say a big thank you.

Daniella Graham (8)

My Mum

My mum is kind, she never minds
My mum is cool, she could swim in the biggest pool
My mum is clever, she's never let me down
My mum is smashing, she's always dashing

My mum is exciting, but always writing
My mum is the best, better than the rest.
My mum cares and loves pears.

My mum's fine but loves a drop of wine
My mum's a star and she could handle a bar
My mum doesn't have a car and the school is very far.

Nana-Akyere Quagraine (8)

My Mum

Thank you Mum, I think you're lovely
You make me all puzzly
You take me places
With your cases and make silly faces

Thank you Mum, I think you're kind
When I'm nutty, you just throw me in a beehive
When I'm angry
You put me upside down

Thank you Mum, I think you're super
Just like Superman
You give me hugs and kisses
And say I'm a missus.

Hamza Osman (8)

My Mum

Thank you Mum for being the best
and being there for me,
Thank you Mum for caring
and loving me.

Thank you Mum for being charming
and always being calming,
Thank you Mum for being kind
and when I'm evil, you never mind.

And all I wanted to say is thank you.

Chloe O'Dwyer (9)

My Mum

My mum is nice and kind to me
My mum plays with me
My mum likes to eat rice,
My mum likes to play with a dice.

I like my mum
My mum likes me
My mum has brown hair
My mum and me like to drink tea.

My mum has curly hair
My mum has light brown eyes
My mum has a baby of eight months
My mum never tells me lies.

My mum washes the dishes
My mum is funny
My mum feeds the fishes
Thank you Mum, I love you!

Daniela Saramago (8)

Thank You Mum

Thank you Mum, I think you're kind
When I am bad, you don't mind
You wash my nose
You iron my clothes

Thank you Mum, I think you're good
You smell just like a flower
Using lots of power
Come outside with me and smell the wood

Thank you Mum, I think you're a good runner
You take me to parties
And let me meet everyone
When we go home you buy me Smarties

Thank you Mum, I think you're loveable
You have lovely clothes
When you get those
I love you, so you are huggable.

Chanice Nembhard (8)

Thank You Mum

Thank you Mum I think you're fantastic
The greatest mum in the world
You help me out at all times
The most helpful mum in the whole
Wide world.

Thank you Mum I love you so much
Thank you Mum you're my favourite mum
The nicest mum in the world
Thank you Mum you're always there for me.

Thank you Mum I love you so much
You are the mum who helps me out
And wakes me up to be ready
Thank you Mum, you help me out when
I'm in trouble.

Timi Akinyemi (8)

This Is The Mum ...

This is the mum who wakes me up,
Gets me out of bed,
Helps me do up my buttons.
My mum is beautiful she is.

This is the mum who makes me tea,
My mum reminds me of stuff,
She even makes me breakfast.
My mum reminds me when I'm going swimming.

This is the mum who is loveable
She washes the dishes
She feeds the fishes and
Takes me out to buy trainers.

This is the mum who makes my packed lunch,
My mum helps me learn my times table,
My mum bakes me cakes.
My mum helps me with my homework.

Berya Mehmet (9)

My Mum

Thank you Mum, I think you're the best,
You wash the dishes, you iron my clothes.
You saved my life from a car crash.

Thank you Mum, I think you're great
You're a super-duper mum
You hoover the house
and clean my brother's nappy.

Thank you Mum, I think you're smashing,
You make my dinner
And do my hair so quickly
I love you Mum, so much.

Laura Aimable (8)

My Mum

My mum is fast
My mum is cool
My mum might run a Christmas ball

My mum is strict
But I don't mind
She also is so very kind

My mum is intelligent
My mum is a cook
My mum lets me go outside
And mostly reads a book

My mum is a superstar
But I call her a pop star
She likes to play music
She doesn't go to the bar.

Denzil Sampson (8)

My Mum Is...

My mum is so wonderful to me
Every time I see her I fill with glee
She is such fun
She shines like the sun

My mum is so sweet
But not to eat
She is so sporty
She tells me off if I'm naughty

My mum is so great
She is like a saint
I love her so much
Because she makes my lunch.

I love my mum.

Bobi Jean Benjamin (8)

My Mum

Thank you Mum, I think you're great,
Every day when you pick me up you wait outside the gate.
When I go to the park I have no friends but I know you're my mate,
Thank you Mum, you're my best friend.

Thank you Mum, every hour I get flowers.
Please don't go, I love you so much.
Mum you're one in a million,
You're the best mum in the world.

We play together, we lay on the bed together.
I will never ever leave you
Mum, I love you so much.
You're great.

Raphael Anene (8)

My Mum

Thank you Mum, you are so kind
Everything I lose you always find
You wash the dishes
And you feed the fishes

This is the mum who is ever so calm
She even has a golden charm
There's no need to be so glum
But you look like a plum.

Patrice McLynn (8)

Mummy

M y mummy is so great,
U nderstanding, never late.
M other, Mother, don't be such a bother.
M itter, whitter but don't be so bitter.
Y es, yes, my mother is so great ... so no need for a debate.
   M u m m y ... spells *mummy*.

Sylvia Anyan-Brown (9)

Mums

M ums take care of us and more.
U gly, horrible, mean, it doesn't matter.
M ums will still care.
S uper, fantastic, great.

T elling you a story,
A hug from her to you.
K ind, loving, generous, so many things to say.
E xtraordinary powers.

C aring for you and for others.
A beautiful woman, inside and out.
R adiant at all times!
E veryone needs their mum.

O versees your life,
F orever your friend.

U nderstands all your problems.
S eeing is believing.

B uying you gifts.
E verlasting love for you.
S o many words to describe mums.
T eaching you good things.

Brittany Dawson

All About My Mum

My mum's face is beautiful like a rose,
My mum has a voice like a fairy.
My mum's hair is lovely and black as the winter mornings.
My mum's lips are smooth like marble.
My mum's eyes are shiny and bright brown.
My mum's clothes are the coolest in the world.
My mum's trainers are the greatest of all.
My mum's hats are the prettiest of all.
My mum's eyebrows are silkiest of all countries.

Saffron McGibbon (9)

Mum

Mum cleans
Mum cooks
Mum makes tea and she loves me.

Mum mopes
Mum wipes
And she cares for me.

Mum makes cakes
Mum puts flowers in the garden
And she thinks about me.

Mum drinks tea
Mum drinks coffee and
She makes stuff for me.

Mum glues
Mum helps
And she makes the
House sparkle

Mum makes eggs
Mum Hoovers the floor
And she does lots of things.

Mum listens to me
Mum has a rest
And she buys me things.

Adnan Sakinsel (8)

My Great Mum

My mum helps me with my homework,
My mum cooks my dinner.
My mum helps me
My mum says goodnight.

My mum cleans up my room,
My mum puts my covers on.
My mum works around the house,
My mum helps to find my stuff.

My mum makes coffee,
My mum likes babies.
My mum likes hamsters,
My mum likes guinea pigs.

Canan Kolcak (8)

My Mum

My mum is a very nice mum
she always feeds my tum.

She cooks very nice food
that makes me in the mood.

She sometimes cooks meat and rice
that is very nice.

My mum cleans my clothes
and tickles my toes.

She looks after me so well
that either here or there, I never fell.

Jordan Messoud

My Mum!

My mum is an unusual lady,
she's busy, hard-working and *crazy!*

She cleans every single day,
I love my mother, hooray!

She'll let me have anything I want,
But she won't let me go search and hunt!

She's a kind, intelligent person,
She may be a little bit boring, mostly fun!

Hooray, hooray! What a wonderful mum,
If you don't believe me, really do so come.

A mother's heart is like a rose!

Shadia Hussain (10)

Celebrating Mums

W akes you up with a
H ug
A sks if she can
T reat you

A lways
L oves you
L istens to you

M orning and night, always
O n call
T o
H ear you
E mbrace you
R escue you and
S poil you

D usts you
O ff when you fall over

B ut best of all, in the
E vening she
S nuggles you down and
T ucks you up tight, in your bed.

Rachel Cable (11)

Mums

Mums are gorgeous
Mums are great
So I think that we should
Celebrate!

They wash, cook, iron and clean
And protect us from those who are mean
They make our beds and wash our hair
And sometimes we forget how much they care

They keep us company through good and bad
And comfort us when we are sad
They never have time to rest
That's why I think that they're the best!

Love your mums
And love them well
Give them a break
And don't make their lives hell

I love my mum loads
I love her lots
So I want to let her know
That she is tops!

Abigail Cotton (11)

Give Them A Break

Mums are gorgeous
Mums are great
They cook our meals,
Without debate.

They make our beds
They clean as well,
They do the polishing,
All is swell.

They are pretty
They are stunning,
They are kind,
But sometimes cunning.

They chase us around,
To be good.
So I think,
That we should,
Take the time to really care,
Because they are all so rare.

Give them a break to let them know,
Just how much you love them so.
Grab a Hoover,
Do the cleaning,
Just look at how much she is beaming.

Throw them a party,
Celebrate!
This is going to be great!
Let them know how much they mean,
Tell them that they look eighteen!

Emma Cook (11)

My Mum

My mum is wonderful,
My mum is never dull,
She is great at cooking,
She always like to hum and sing,
She always helps when I have a frown,
She turns them all upside down.
My mum has lots of old friends,
Her conversations never end,
She loves to shop for bargains,
Bringing home all sorts of things.
I don't think my mum would cope,
If it wasn't for all her 'soaps'.
'Corrie', 'EastEnders' and 'Emmerdale',
Putting a smile on her face without fail.
My mum also loves to drink coffee,
But the person who makes it, is always me!
My mum is wonderful
My mum is brill.
My mum is great,
Let's *celebrate!*

Amy Brown (12)

Mum

There is a lady called Marie,
She's loving, she's bright, she's pretty.
She's always been there,
To love and to care,
And she is my beautiful mummy.

She's always had kindness to share,
Especially when life seems unfair.
She looks straight at me,
I'm soon filled with glee,
For me she has always been there.

When her smiley face starts to glow,
Both of our hearts start to know,
Our love will not wane,
No gloom will remain,
All my sadness will simply go.

Now she really deserves a good rest,
As she's passed every going test.
I'd like to thank Mum
For all that she's done,
I'd like her to know she's the best.

Sinead Cleaver (11)

Yes, That's My Mum

Mum number one for sale ...
She tidies your room
With a brand new broom
Price: £125,000.
No, that's not *my* mum!

Mum number two for sale ...
She washes the dishes,
Fulfils all your wishes
Price: £250,000.
No, that's not *my* mum!

Mum number three for sale ...
She goes to Tesco,
But what for? I don't know.
Price: £1,000,000.
No, that's not *my* mum!

Mum number four for sale ...
She's the one,
She's the super mum,
Price: less.
Yes, that's my mum!

Sana Chaudhry (12)

Mums

Mums, why are they here?
They emit a glow, when you're near.
They give lots of attention,
They deserve a public mention.
When they ask you to tidy your room,
Then they are full of gloom!
But who cares about that?
I don't, so chew on that!
There are different types of mothers.
Some are arty, some write for book covers!
Some are musical, some are not.
Of mum types, there are a lot!
But to me, mine's the best in the world!
She is a pianist, and her hair is curled.
So let's sing this little rhyme:
Two, four, six, eight,
Who do we appreciate?
Mums, cos they're *great!*

Hannah Bradford (11)

I Love You Mum

Thanks for showing
Throughout my life
Help and support
Through all my strife.

Thanks for showing
Since my birth
That you loved me more
Than all this Earth.

Thanks for showing
Through all my years
That you would help
Overcome my fears.

Thanks for showing
Since that winter's day
That your love for me
Would never stray.

I've loved you, Mum,
Since my first blink.
Unlike the Titanic,
Our love won't sink.

Catherine Bowering (11)

My Mum's Cool!

My mum is really cool,
She's never late picking me up from school.
She's always there at three o'clock,
Not five-past three, on the dot.

My mum is really kind,
The bestest mum you'd ever find.
She takes me out and buys me things,
And lets me answer when the phone rings.

My mum is really fun,
We make cakes and currant buns.
She tells me jokes and makes me laugh,
And always gives me the biggest half.

She does have her off days,
But I don't mind,
She's mostly always great, I find.

My mum is always there,
To wash my socks and comb my hair,
But better than that and most of all,
My mum will always care.

Amy Breakwell (12)

Mums

Mums go back through decades,
Centuries and millenniums too,
They're loyal, faithful and cuddly,
And they'll always look after you!

But they also have a dark side
When you step out of line,
They'll send you to bed early,
If you whinge and whine.

They cook and clean and care for you,
And work hard all day long.
They're mostly very happy
And fill the world with song.

So always pay attention,
Because in our later years,
We'll find their advice useful
To wipe away our tears.

Mums go back through decades,
Centuries and millenniums too,
And before we even know it,
The mums will be me and you!

Rosie Dowd-Smyth (11)

My Multi-Purpose Mum

My mum, how do I describe her?
The memories we have shared together
Seem to be in a bit of a blur.
She is snazzy and sweet,
But not exactly petite.
Still, her heart is fragile enough;
Winning her over is hard, if she is in a huff.
You can easily convince her though,
Just assure her and she will go easily with the flow.
She loves cooking and I love her food.
She loves telling me off and I enjoy being told off
When we do make up eventually,
I grab anything I can scoff,
Before we start arguing about something again quickly.
Every day she shows her motherly love and her devilish anger.
Every day I try to show my daughterly affection to keep myself out of danger.
We have a love and hate relationship,
Like most friends do,
In fact, I like my world, which mainly consists of us two.
We've seen good times and we've seen bad times too,
That fact gives us yet another excuse to argue.
Now do cheer up and don't look so glum,
Because today I thank you, for being my multi-purpose mum!

Madeeha Ahmed (16)

Young Writers Information

We hope you have enjoyed reading this book - and that you will continue to enjoy it in the coming years.
If you like reading and writing poetry and short stories drop us a line, or give us a call, and we'll send you a free information pack. Alternatively, if you would like to order further copies of this book or any of our other titles, then please give us a call or log onto our website at **www.youngwriters.co.uk**

Young Writers, Remus House, Coltsfoot Drive, Woodston, Peterborough PE2 9JX
Tel (01733) 890066
Email youngwriters@forwardpress.co.uk